Photographs by E. Alan McGee
Introduction by Yolande Gwin

Published by Perry Communications, Inc.
Atlanta, Georgia

"ATLANTA AT HOME"

Copyright 1979 by The Auxiliary of Henrietta Egleston Hospital for Children, Inc.
1405 Clifton Road, N. E.
Atlanta, Georgia 30322

Publisher and Printer: Perry Communications, Inc.
2181 Sylvan Road, S. W.
Atlanta, Georgia 30344

All rights reserved, including the rights of reproduction and use in any form or by any means, including the making of copies by any photo process, or by any mechanical or electronic device, printed or written or oral, or recording for sound or visual reproduction or for use in any knowledge or retrieval system or device, unless permission in writing is obtained beforehand from the copyright holder or its authorized representative.

First Edition: August, 1979

The Henrietta Egleston Hospital for Children
A Love Story

The Henrietta Egleston Hospital for Children

by Yolande Gwin

This is a love story.

The Story starts with a man who had a generous heart, and his gift to Atlanta, a children's hospital. The man is gone now, but his memory lives in the hospital, which is this year celebrating its Fiftieth Anniversary.

Having achieved high rank on the national scene, Egleston is one of the heartbeats of Atlanta. Each of the fifty years has brought meaningful advances in fine medical care. Each year has found Atlantans giving their money, time and talents to support the good work of the hospital and to further its goals.

So turn back the pages of time to 1870. Atlanta was active, rebuilding the destructions of the Civil War. Arriving in Atlanta, along with other thousands, was a young family. Mr. and Mrs. Thomas Egleston came from Charleston, bringing their young children, Thomas, Jr., Daniel, Theodore, and Henrietta. Another little son, Clarence, had died in Charleston. The hope of finding happiness in a new city was shattered. Tragedy struck. The younger children died of tuberculosis. Only Thomas survived.

The sadness that the young boy experienced in seeing his mother care for and lose her children stayed with Thomas all his life. In those days, a child stayed at home to survive or die. The toll was terrible. Thomas' heart went out to his mother and to others like her.

A bright boy, Thomas found a job at fourteen, and he amassed a fortune before he died at age sixty in 1916. During his business years his financial assets grew and grew, and he dreamed of a hospital for children, where even those whose parents were unable to pay could receive the care they needed. At that time, there were children's hospitals in Boston and Philadelphia, but none in the still war-scarred South. In his will, Thomas Egleston gave one hundred thousand dollars to build a hospital for children. It was the largest single benefaction for a non-sectarian charity ever established to that date in Atlanta. The hospital was to be named for his mother, The Henrietta Egleston Hospital for Children.

Thomas Egleston's will asked his friends Judge Alex C. King, Mr. William R. Prescott, Dr. W.W. Memminger, rector of All Saints Episcopal Church, and Egleston's cousin, Beverly DuBose, to work with the Trust Company of Georgia and his trusted friend W.E. Chapin, as representative, to carry out his bequest.

These men, all with keen business minds, invested the money until a suitable site could be found for the hospital. The times were critical, America was at war, building costs were soaring, and money was tight. In their minds they thought it best to wait.

Three years after Egleston's death, in 1919, they decided to buy the Calvin W. Hunnicutt home on Spring Street, just opposite Baltimore Block. The street was paved with rugged Belgium bricks. Atlanta was growing, traffic was getting thicker and louder. Even the paving blocks added to the noise. The men decided that this was no place for a

Thomas Egleston

children's hospital after all. Lady Luck seems to have taken a hand. They sold the house, making a profit of sixty thousand dollars. By 1926, the original one hundred thousand dollar bequest had grown to two hundred thousand. Lady Luck led the trustees to Forrest Road. Fifteen acres of land, situated in what was then the center of Atlanta's population, was available from the Gardner family, old Atlanta landowners.

A site for the hospital had at last been found, but projected operating costs had risen to fifty thousand dollars a year. Ten years after Egleston's original bequest, the hospital still seemed an impossible dream. The businessmen shook their heads, but the women who had seen this idea flower wanted to see the reality. "Please, go ahead," they said. "We're willing to help." An SOS went from William Prescott to his friend, Dr. Dan Elkin, chief of surgery at Emory University Hospital. From Elkin went another SOS to architect Robert Dillon. Design a hospital for children, he was told. Put life and love into it, and hurry!

Doctor Hines Roberts

Nurse Jessie Candlish

Dillon began a cross country search for ideas, which he would combine to make Egleston the most modern and best equipped for the day. With him on this trip was Dr. Hines Roberts, whom Dr. Elkin had chosen as the medical director of the hospital. As the men traveled and planned, Dr. Roberts suggested that the hospital's exterior be patterned after the famous "Innocenti Hospital" in Florence, Italy, designed by Brunelleschi in the 15th Century. So the plans grew from there. A stucco facade with arches and a typical Italianate red-tiled roof were the motif. Medallions, copies of the Della Robbia plaques on the Florentine hospital, were incorporated. The plaques, showing an infant with outstretched arms, have become the symbol of the hospital and appear on its Christmas seals each year.

Meanwhile, Dr. Hines Roberts, who was to serve as the self-sacrificing and inspiring head of medicine at Egleston for thirty-one years, was choosing his pediatric staff. They were Dr. Lewis Hoppe, Dr. T. Bolling Gay and Dr. William Funkhouser.

Something was missing. An administrator or director of nursing. It took the doctors two years to find the right person. They finally persuaded a woman who in the years to come was to be one of the leading forces of the hospital. Her name, Jessie Maria Candlish of Pembrokshire, South Wales. Her background included studies at the Children's Hospital in Baltimore. Strict and direct, she was forty-nine when she agreed to supervise this hospital, not yet built. As proved through the many years she dedicated to its work, Egleston Hospital could not have been more fortunate in this choice.

The hospital opened in October, 1928. About six hundred children received care during the first year.

It was a wonderful beginning.

There was work to do to keep the hospital functioning and growing. Five women met at the home of Mrs. William Prescott. As the wife of the trustee most concerned with the hospital from the beginning, Mrs. Prescott had early seen the need for a supporting organization.

Thirty-nine women agreed to pledge their support, and the first Auxiliary was formed, with Mrs. Prescott and Mrs. Frank Holland as the first presidents. In the early years they sewed for the children and staff, making diapers and bibs as well as surgical masks and gowns. They collected mother's milk for the incubator babies. Fourteen church "circles," representing every denomination then in Atlanta, contributed hours of sewing.

It was realized very quickly that the Auxiliary would need money. How to raise it? Someone had a whimsical idea that appealed to everyone. The "Pet Parade" was perfect for a children's hospital. Mrs. Stacy E. Hill and Yolande Gwin organized the first one. Asa G. Candler, Jr., agreed to show his pet elephant. Other entries were a possum, a pair of turtles, a talking whippet and a thirty-five year old white horse!

The "Pet Parade" provided great fun for all and good profits. Looking around for other projects, the Auxiliary considered ways they could continue to raise money. Mrs. Jesse Draper and Mrs. Lelia Dangerfield had a great idea. They planned the sponsorship of a tour of Atlanta gardens, patterned after tours they had enjoyed in Virginia. Little did they know what a gold mine they had found! The tour became the greatest money-making project the Auxiliary has sponsored through the years.

The first tours were gardens only. Admission was a dollar and half for ten gardens. Little Boy and Girl Scouts in uniform served as ushers, as hundreds of

Atlantans from all sectors of the city visited the beautiful English formal gardens and woodland gardens, spruced up for the occasion. In a few years, house and garden tours replaced the all-garden idea, and the event, at the height of the dogwood bloom, heralded the beginning of spring each year. Except for the years during the Second World War, when austerity was the mode, the Spring Tour of Homes has brought in much needed money for the hospital.

Egleston has always inspired support. In 1933, the Service Group was formed to assist the needy in Atlanta. The home of Mrs. Edward Inman hosted the first meeting, and it was decided to contribute towards the maintenance of several beds at Egleston Hospital. An Omnibus Sale was their undertaking, and they sold everything from worn-out tennis shoes to broken lamps. It's hard to imagine such an idea even being discussed in the beautiful rooms at Swan House! The Candler and Massell families lent empty building spaces for these sales, and they lasted for one month. By 1958, the Service Group had merged with the Egleston Auxiliary and devoted all of its energies to helping the little patients at the hospital.

Another supporting group had its foundation in 1928, the year the hospital opened. The Cherokee Garden Club, aware that the children could be helped to health by beauty and nature, brought plants and shrubs from their own yards to fill a new garden planned by landscape architect Norman Butts. A special rose garden was dedicated to Dollie Blalock Black. Almost overnight, a red clay tract was a spot of fairyland where the children could visit and play. Other garden clubs joined in. Before long, members of the Peachtree and Colonial clubs had work underway. During the forties when food was rationed, Constance Draper suggested to her friend Laurie Davis Webster that something could be done to raise vegetables for the children at the hospital. A demonstration garden, open to the public, was the result of much hard labor and lots of help. School children around the town contributed bricks for a retaining wall. The story of the garden was carried in newspapers all over the country. The Garden Club of America gave Mrs. Webster its highest award, "for creative and practical work." Best of all, there were twenty terraces of raspberries, strawberries and every kind of vegetable, including plenty of pumpkins for Halloween!

The Camellia Show, sponsored by the Peachtree Garden Club, was another fund-raiser. In 1946, the Biltmore Hotel Ballroom was the scene of a fabulous display of this flower, so beloved by Southerners, in all its varieties. Part of the proceeds from the first show brought a beautiful iron gate to ornament the garden.

The Atlanta Junior League had been helpful to Egleston since the early years of the Auxiliary, sewing doctor's robes, blankets, sheets and pillow cases, meeting in a "loaned" room at the Georgian Terrace Hotel. League volunteers went to the hospital to help some of the children with their schoolwork and found other volunteer duties, such as writing

Constance Knowles Draper

letters for the children, taking them for walks in the garden and making things merry when time for Santa came. Many League members make Egleston the site for their volunteer hours, now, each year.

As Atlanta grew and changed, William Prescott, who had guided the development of the hospital since Thomas Egleston's bequest, asked banker John Sibley, Chairman of the Board of the Trust Company of Georgia, to take over his duties. The time had come when the 50-bed hospital was too small to meet the needs of the city. Even though the task seemed impossible, it was decided that the hospital would have to move. Charles Kellstadt, Board of Trustees member and head of Atlanta's Sears Roebuck, was tapped by John Sibley to tour America to study the planning and operation of a modern children's hospital. Egleston had to be a 100-bed hospital, with facilities for teaching and for research. But move the hospital? So many people had put devotion into the work of the building on

Forrest Avenue and the thought of moving sick children was appalling. Dr. Hines Roberts, Dr. Phinizy Calhoun and Dr. Lon Grove studied the situation and agreed. It had to be done. Then, help came from an unexpected source.

Mrs. Mary Finley was the widow of Samuel E. Finley who had served on the Board of Trustees of the hospital. Both Finleys knew the needs of the hospital. Mrs. Finley provided in her will for more than a million dollars for those needs, two-thirds for the construction of a new building and one-third for its operation. All of her furnishings were left to the Junior League, to be auctioned for the benefit of the hospital. Then there came a grant from the Emily and Ernest Woodruff Foundation, and a gift from the family of John Goddard. At that time, Emory University gave five acres along Clifton Road, across from the University Hospital, and the future of the new Egleston Hospital was assured. Emory and Egleston remain two separate but sister hospitals, Egleston supplying the pediatric beds for the larger hospital, and the Emory University Department of Pediatrics supplying the professional direction of services to patients. Trustees John O. Chiles and Boisfeuillet Jones, with Richard Blumberg, M.D., Chairman of Pediatrics for Emory, demanded a strong man as chief physician. Joseph Patterson had a notable background and was chosen as the man for the job. Since that year, 1959, he has been the leader, innovator, teacher and friend that the hospital needed to remain great. He has inspired many young men and women to follow his example, and served as a counselor

Nurse and patient

to patients and their families. Gilbert McLemore was selected as hospital administrator and served from 1959 to 1976. Always the personable gentleman, he made many lifelong friends for the hospital. Other key figures at the time of Egleston's move were Dr. William Mitchell, Dr. Ellsworth Cole and Dr. W.L. Funkhouser.

The staff now comprises over 300 doctors and dentists from the metropolitan area. In addition, there are over 400 full-time and part-time employees. Over 600 volunteer workers, from the hospital auxiliary and other groups, give more than 13,000 hours of service a year!

The contract for the new hospital was signed by Charles Kellstadt, Howard Candler, Dr. Goodrich White and John Sibley. Dedication of the new hospital was January 12, 1959, and Atlanta opened her arms and heart as before. Miss Jessie Candlish, always on the scene, helped carry the little patients to their new hospital rooms. This devoted nurse, always supported by her faithful staff, especially orderly "Doctor" Rufus Johnson, engineer John Bickers and housekeeper Clyde McKinney, seemed to tire on those moving days. The hospital staff and her many friends suggested that she step down from her strenuous and demanding job and become Director of Volunteers. She agreed and was happy to know that her successor would be an outstanding nurse Margaret Bodeker. Twenty years before, she had been a student nurse at Egleston and found an inspiration that could never die in the teaching of "Miss Jessie." During the war, she had served with the Emory Unit from North Africa to France. After studies at Harvard, she had returned to Egleston.

New building, new equipment, new goals, new challenges. The Auxiliary rose to the occasion. A Cotton Cotillion was held to raise money for the hospital, and then in 1960, the Bal de Salut became a reality.

Mrs. Ivan Allen, Jr., and a group of her friends decided to sponsor an annual presentation ball for members of the Atlanta Debutante Club. Egleston receives the proceeds from each June "Bal." Each year more beautiful than the last, the "Bal" has as its most exciting moment the welcome from the previous year's debutantes to the new. Ivan Allen, Jr., traditionally introduces each girl and her escort. Then the officers of the debutante club, elected by the members, are announced. The ballroom seems to glow with youth and beauty as the dancing begins. It's a wonderful occasion, for a wonderful cause!

There are many Atlanta families which have succumbed to a mania nick-named "The Egleston Syndrome." The symptoms of this condition are years of devotion and unselfish loyalty plus a determination to do all they can to help this little hospital, and the "Syndrome" can be said to be passed from generation to generation.

Some of the families who have caught the fever are the Beverly DuBoses, Sr., and their children Mr. and Mrs. Beverly M. DuBose, Jr., and Betty DuBose Skiles, and now the third generation, which includes Dean DuBose Smith, Auxiliary President-elect.

Mr. and Mrs. William Prescott were of course early victims of the "E.S.," and their granddaughter, Mrs. Clayton (Sally Prescott) Rich carries on their tradition.

Mrs. Bolling Jones and her sister, Nell Hodgson Woodruff and her husband, Robert Woodruff, have certainly been "Egleston People." The George Woodruffs and daughters Frances, Jane and Irene, and in the third generation, Mrs. F.M. (Irene Michael) Bird, Jr., and Mrs. Charles (Missy Woodruff) Werk have caught the fever.

Mrs. Edward Albert Thornton and her nieces, Mrs. Alfred Kennedy, Jr. and her daughter Ginger Kennedy Epstein and Mrs. Thornton Kennedy have given so many proofs of love that they might be considered "carriers" of the Egleston Syndrome. John O. Chiles was an ebullient personality who worked to help the hospital, and his daughter Nona Chiles McDuffie contracted the benevolent obsession and served as a Bal de Salut chairman with characteristic flair.

John H. Harland handed on the "E.S.," along with his Irish twinkle to John and "Bimby" Harland Conant. This kind of devotion, so imbued in these and many other Atlanta families, is apparent when talking with three ladies who have worked as Auxiliary members and hospital volunteers for fifty-one years (each!). Mrs. Hines Roberts, Mrs. Bolling Jones and Mrs. Lewis Hoppe. During a recognition ceremony, one of them (we'll never tell) said, "You know we volunteers don't do this work for praise, but it's kind of like putting a little manure on your flower garden. It doesn't hurt a bit!"

I hope the "Egleston Syndrome" keeps spreading and a cure is never found!

Through the years the hospital has grown in spirit, and each year seems to bring new talent to its volunteer projects. Mrs. Blake Van Leer served for many years as Volunteer Chairman. Under her banner, women of all ages gave many hours of love to the children. The Auxiliary welcomed the help of other organizations in its yearly project, the Tour of Homes. In 1977, a new money-making project, the brain child of Mrs. Earl Patton, was born. A Christmas Festival of Trees, held in mid-November, had trees and decorations for everyone to enjoy and take home. This was combined with the Christmas Bazaar, long an enjoyable and profitable part of the Auxiliary's work.

And now the half-century mark is passing. The hospital is once more at an important turning point. The 100-bed structure built in 1959 is no longer adequate for today's demands for patient care and advancing technology.

Old Egleston Hospital

The Board of Trustees, chaired by Alfred E. Boylston, Jr., and counseled by new hospital administrator Selena D. Dunn and Chief Physician Dr. Joseph H. Patterson, has proposed and received approval for a major expansion/renovation of the hospital. This new project will begin late in this 50th Anniversary year.

Its completion, in 1982, will enable the hospital to treat children from all over the Southeastern United States. The number of children will be more than eight thousand in a year.

The hospital is completely non-profit and every year depends on the generosity of the community to help bear the expenses of the many non-paying patients who seek medical help.

This book of beautiful homes is one more of the fund-raising projects which the faithful Auxiliary continues to conduct. The fact that you have purchased it makes you a part owner of Thomas Egleston's dream and a participant in one of Atlanta's greatest love stories.

Since 1933, the year of the first Tour of Homes for the Henrietta Egleston Children's Hospital, Atlanta's skyline and boundaries have undergone a complete change. However, despite the progress of the last fifty years, the city's tree-shaded residential streets remain mostly intact. It is true that parts of Peachtree Road, which used to be lined with stately houses, have become commercialized and that the fast-food stands and filling stations bring sadness to the hearts of those who remember that earlier time. But Paces Ferry Road and Tuxedo Park, Haynes Manor and Peachtree Heights still beckon delighted visitors and proud Atlantans to drive the winding roads and admire the dogwood and spring flowers.

This section of the book tells about some of the houses that have fallen victim to or have been saved from our changing times. Typical casualties of progress, often because of the philanthropy of their owners, include the Haverty and Slaton mansions on Peachtree Road and the Maddox house on Paces Ferry Road. These old places, remembered by three generations of kin and friends, are gone.

Other houses that have been of great interest on the hospital tours are now changed but still around. They have become clubs, museums or schools. A few pictured here have been restored by new owners for a more modern life-style. Several others have an uneasy future. They await a buyer with a king's ransom or the wrecker's ball.

"Woodhaven," home of Mr. and Mrs. Robert F. Maddox, on West Paces Ferry Road was originally a summer house before a paved road, electric lights, or running water reached this section, now considered "close-in." The house was built in 1911 on a wooded tract of 76 acres. The Georgia Governor's Mansion has replaced the original house. The amphitheatre and gardens still exist, but horses no longer pull the lawnmowers.

In its heyday, the "Maddox Place" provided an opulent setting for a reception for Metropolitan Opera stars in a marble conservatory with bubbling fountains. There was also a completely furnished playhouse with a working stove. Photo: Courtesy Mrs. John R. Maddox, Mrs. Edward D. Smith

Far "Out Peachtree," meaning then north of downtown, was the home of the James J. Haverty family. Mrs. Haverty's maiden name was Clare Malone, and both Mr. and Mrs. Haverty were proud of their descent from families of County Clare in Ireland. The property was enclosed with a hand-forged iron fence, and the gates proclaimed the name, "Villa Clare."

An old rock quarry near the rear of the nine-acre property was converted into a sunken garden with many terraces. The quarry had served as a Confederate breastworks during the seige of Atlanta.

President Franklin D. Roosevelt appointed Mr. Haverty Chairman of Fine Arts in Georgia. Under his aegis, the Cyclorama was renovated. Atlanta wildlife artist Athos Menaboni was a protégé. Mr. Haverty's collection of American and European art is now housed in the High Museum.
Photo: Courtesy The Atlanta Speech School

The old John Ogden home on West Paces Ferry Road, now the main hall of private school Pace Academy, looks today much as it did when it was shown on the Tour of Homes in 1935.
Photo: E. Alan McGee

The former home of Mr. and Mrs. Frank Lamar Fleming recalls the march of splendid houses that once gave Peachtree Road its cachet. It still reflects the charm of a bygone era. The English Tudor style house was completed in 1917. Hand-craftsmanship of the time is preserved in its carved paneling and limestone mantels.

The grounds had a unique collection of native Southern azaleas which have recently been donated and moved to the woodlands surrounding the Atlanta Historical Society. There they give springtime pleasure to Atlantans and visitors. Admission to the gardens is free.
Photo: Courtesy Mrs. Robert L. Garges

Built during the Colonial Revival of the 1930's, the Alexander house was originally on a beautiful drive of trees extending 1,500 feet from Peachtree. The front property is now Phipps Plaza shopping mall, but the house remains.

Mr. Henry A. Alexander was born in 1874, a descendant of a Jewish family that came to America in 1608. The house was called "Peniel" from Genesis 32:30: "...and Jacob called the place Peniel; for I have seen God face to face, and my life is preserved."

The house has beautiful woodwork and carvings, and the family allowed it to be used as the first Decorator's Showhouse to benefit the Atlanta Symphony Orchestra.
Photo: Courtesy Miss Judith Alexander

Because the red-tile roof, when wet with rain, seemed to give off multicolored shimmers of light, the owners of this house rather whimsically named it "Rainbow Terrace." Now empty—some say haunted—boarded-up and dilapidated, the house carries a ghostly aspect which is saddening.

Still called the "Heinz House," although it has had subsequent owners, the house was designed about 1920 for Atlanta banker Henry Heinz and his wife Lucy Candler Owens, who was the only daughter of the "Coca-Cola King" Asa G. Candler. An intruder shot and killed Mr. Heinz in 1943. This tragedy —so incongruous to the beautiful mansion shaded with huge trees and lacy with dogwood in the spring— created a spirit of fear in an Atlanta then accustomed to sleeping with doors unlocked. The house stands as a reminder of a simpler, happier day.
Photo: Courtesy Mrs. William D. Owens and Mrs. W. Davis Owens, Jr.

Set back 600 feet from West Paces Ferry Road, the home of Mr. and Mrs. John William Grant, Jr., is now the Cherokee Town and Country Club. Construction was begun in 1914, and the house was completed in 1917. It was designed by architect Walter T. Downing and styled after the Grant castle in Scotland near Grantown-on-Spey. The Grants called it "Craigellechie" from a Scotch word meaning "a clan gathering place." One hundred and fifty acres of natural woodland surrounded the house, a lake and a tennis court. The music room, now the clubhouse bar, had furniture made of green satinwood, including the cabinet for the Victrola.
Photo: Courtesy Atlanta Historical Society

Dr. and Mrs. F. Phinizy Calhoun were considered local pioneers when they purchased 7-1/2 acres in a new area being developed by Eratus Rivers around 1910. They built a Tudor style house of 24 rooms and originally named it "Shadow Hill" but changed to a name celebrating their Scotch ancestry, "Rossdhu," from the home of the Colquhoun clan on Loch Lomond.

Mrs. Calhoun was Marion Peel, from a noted Atlanta family, and her hobby was growing camellias. Gathering friends who shared her interest in flowers, she was one of the founders of the city's oldest garden club, naturally named "The Peachtree Garden Club." The house is now a school.
Photo: Courtesy Mrs. F. Phinizy Calhoun, Jr.

"Swan House" has been open to the public since 1967, and it is owned and carefully maintained by the Atlanta Historical Society. Despite its magnificence, it was the very private domain of one family, the Inmans. Edward Inman was the son of Hugh T. Inman who amassed a fortune as a cotton broker after the Civil War. After Princeton, Edward married Emily MacDougald of Columbus in 1901. The couple loved to travel, and after many trips to Europe and in this country, they decided to build a house to contain the furnishings and art that they had collected.

"Swan House," designed by Philip Shutze in the manner of Palladio, invokes the spirit of villas in the cool, wooded hills near Venice. Furnished now exactly as it was kept by the Inmans, the house is open Tuesday through Saturday from 10:30 to 4:30, and on Sunday from 2:00 to 4:30.
Photo: Courtesy E. Alan McGee

Home of the Andrew Calhouns, this Italian baroque villa with the unlikely Scottish name of "Trygveson" was designed by Philip Shutze in the early Twenties. It was inspired by Renaissance villas near Rome, but somehow its opulence in a Georgia landscape suggests the richness of the F. Scott Fitzgerald era.

Atlantans called the house the "Pink Castle," and, on moonlit nights, its stucco gateposts, with a view of the house rising in the distance from terraced gardens, became a favorite rendezvous for the young.

This wonderful house was for a time empty and vandalized. Later, the 18-acre property was subdivided. Now, once again, a prominent Atlanta family live there. The Allison Thornwells have decorated with flair and enjoy "living in a castle."
Photo: Courtesy Atlanta Historical Society

The beautiful English Regency house on Paces Ferry Road near Cherokee Club was designed by Philip Shutze for Mr. and Mrs. Albert Thornton and built in 1938. The façade and turning court landscaping was designed by Edith Henderson, and landscape architect Edward Daugherty created the plans for the beautiful gardens. Edith Hills was the interior designer.

Having no children, Mrs. Thornton dedicated her life to the welfare of others, and Egleston Children's Hospital was one of her prime concerns.

This handsomely dignified house has recently been purchased by Mr. and Mrs. Frank C. Jones.
Photo: Courtesy Trust Department, First National Bank

A happy ending to this chapter on "Atlanta Then," this charming Colonial home of Mrs. Catherine Erwin Maynard was saved from the advance of progress about ten years ago. Designed by Philip Shutze and originally built on Mount Paran Road in 1936, it was moved to its present location on Glen Arden when a highway was planned to cut through the property.

The house contains family heirlooms of four generations, including six mantels and molding from an earlier family home in New Jersey. Now gracefully settled on its new site, it radiates a special charm.
Photo: Courtesy Mrs. Catherine Erwin Maynard

The formal garden, designed by architect/first-owner Hal P. Hentz, is edged with boxwood. The clipped hedges are Burfordi holly. It's a year-round garden, where camellias bloom in January, dogwoods and azaleas in April, hydrangeas and day lilies in June. The summer months yield vegetables planted by the young owners, Mr. and Mrs. Howard Jackson Morrison, Jr., in the inner beds.

Camellia designs, all different one from the other, are seen on the needlepoint chair seats. Executed by Mrs.

Morrison and Mrs. Mary Comer Lane, Mr. Morrison's grandmother, the designs were copied from camellias growing at Lebanon Plantation, Savannah, Mr. Morrison's family home.

The Morrison home was owned for many years by ebullient Atlanta banker Mills B. Lane, uncle of Mr. Morrison. Southern Architectural Review for June, 1937, featured this home and its view of the dining room, seen immediately on entering the foyer. Creamy moiré curtains and wall covering complement the French Regency wallpaper of the foyer.

The E. Reginald Hancock house, built as a Georgian structure in 1922, was later remodeled and given a Greek revival façade. A formal boxwood garden gives way to five acres of woodland bridle paths.

The traditional interior is exemplified by the formal dining room. A Waterford chandelier casts soft light on a table set for company. Bowls of fresh, perfect peaches and shiny magnolia leaves counterpoint the formal, hand-painted china with elegant simplicity.

Dark moulding and wainscoting frames a delicate Chinese wallpaper design of tortoises and cranes.

"Haw Wood" is the fanciful name of this warm and seemingly very old house in a wooded setting. Much younger than its apparent years, it is built of old brick and designed to resemble early homes in Virginia. Combining photographs made by the original owners on trips into the Tidewater area, the architect, John LeBey, created a synthesis of Virginia houses. Joe Walker was the builder. The chimneys are copied from the Saint George Tucker house in Williamsburg. The

windows are taken from those at Westover Plantation.

Real imports from Virginia are the boxwood, started as small plants, now grown to maturity through careful nurturing.

The brick for the attractively curved walk was also made in Virginia. The curve, not typical of 18th Century gardens, follows the contour of the lawn and makes the walk to the house more interesting. Such hand-drawn curves are a favorite device of landscape designer Edith Henderson.

A white, Georgian house with magnolias and a low stone wall is home for Mr. and Mrs. Louis Regenstein. In their library, artist Lamar Dodd's "Sun" rises to light the radiant yellow paneled walls. Yellow is also the background color of the crewel fabric on the chairs that flank the sofa.

Bookshelves abound in this comfortable room, and they show off antique blue and white porcelains in addition to many handsome volumes. Blue geometric embroidered velvet covers the expansive lounge chair and the armchairs that surround the game table. Another shading of blue velvet is used on the occasional chair with its colorful needlework pillow. The use of blue is a natural, coming from the old Chinese rug with its triple medallions, and the apricot of these medallions is the background of another Chinese rug under the card table.

Brilliant turquoise is brought into the room by the lovely Chinese cabinet, and still more color is added by the view of the pool with its surrounding patio. Contemporary porcelains hung above the large window and a number of cloisonné pieces enrich the palette of the room, while Robert Vickery's "Clown" adds to the total cheerfulness. Other highlights are introduced by the dulcimer, the Oriental étagère, and the garden seat stand of the cache pot with its Ming aralia.

A broad blanket of azaleas turns the lawn of Mrs. Fred Patterson's classic Georgian home into a blaze of springtime color.

Espaliered sasanqua camellias line each arch of the enclosed patio garden in the rear. Paths of old brick laid in a basket weave pattern come together to form a sunny terrace between boxwood-lined tulip beds. This formal garden provides an ordered contrast to the wooded areas surrounding the house.

Atlanta architect Henri V. Jova is endowed with a proliferation of talents. Foremost an architect—his firm designed the Colony Square hotel/apartment/office complex—he is well-known as a painter and a designer. Mr. Jova is also credited as the force behind the restoration of Midtown, a neighborhood developed around the turn of the century which had begun to show signs of urban blight. His new Midtown townhouse is, in a way, a sampling of his many facets.

"Mango," a bold abstract painting by

Mr. Jova, dominates the living room. The carved Georgian table below holds a group of 17th Century Chinese artifacts whose intricacies are matched by the natural coral and shell shapes displayed with them. Bright sofa pillows and the sunburst pattern in the quilt pick up the painting's colors.

In the breakfast area, a painting by J.O. Mahoney in muted browns and greys is reflected in the tones of a cabinet server. Bright fruit and flower arrangements add touches of color to the room.

As the officially designated historian of Atlanta and Fulton County, Franklin Miller Garrett keeps several projects going simultaneously and "rambles" from one to the other of two libraries in his home. The larger offers two work areas—a large flat-top desk and a walnut cylinder desk of the 1850s.

Prints, photographs, books, maps and memorabilia attest to Mr. Garrett's many interests, including railroads, ships, the Civil War and the histories of cities.

The original watercolors are part of a series Mr. Garrett commissioned from the late Wilbur G. Kurtz on the early days of Atlanta. The series was begun in 1939, but due to the advent of World War II, took 10 years to complete.

Mr. Garrett is the author of Atlanta and Environs, a two-volume history of the city, and of a later picture history, Yesterday's Atlanta. The 18th century Chippendale architect's desk and corner chair in his smaller "Atlanta room" make a fine ensemble for the writing and compiling that attend such undertakings.

Seen across an open meadow, the house of Mr. and Mrs. Thomas E. Martin, Jr., recalls Tidewater, Virginia and the Colonial era.

In the living room, windowpanes set "twelve over twelve" are framed by interior shutters. An Oushak rug dictates the golds and apricots used in upholstery fabrics. The handsome broken pediment secretary displays a portion of Mrs. Martin's porcelain collection.

An intricately carved pair of Louis XVI overdoors, which once gave entrance to an elegant Parisian salon, now grace the entrance hall of the William Benton house. Interior designer David Byers whose credits include several rooms in the White House, had originally intended to use the overdoors as headboards for beds in the Benton guestroom, but discovered that by an incredible stroke of luck they fit pre-existing spaces and could fulfill their original function.

Traditional furnishings and appointments fit with comfort and ease into this contemporary house designed by Atlanta architect Henri Jova. A skylight, gives daytime illumination, and an antique French chandelier of bronze doré and crystal adds drama.

In contrast, a modern portrait of the Bentons' daughters, Isabelle, Alice and Elizabeth, is actually a sepia drawing on paper. Artist George Beattie made the lightly hatched drawing and devised a way to treat it so that the usual heavy glass frame could be eliminated.

An antique Shiraz rug in the entrance hall and a warm Mahal in the dining room soften floors of russet Saint Joe brick, sealed and waxed to bring out their color. Furniture in the entrance hall and dining room is English, of the 18th and early 19th centuries. Accessories include a large Chinese Export punch bowl and a pair of amber and crystal candelabra in the entry, and a collection of porcelains in the dining room corner cupboard and on the Regency serving cabinet.

Atlanta architect John R. Barnett designed a contemporary multi-level home for Mr. and Mrs. Robert L. Steed that features rough-sawn cedar siding and a natural granite wall. One of the truly unusual features is the bridged entry leading to the foyer lighted by a stained glass window.

Large glass areas add a feeling of lightness to this house, which was sited by the architect to take full advantage of the heavily wooded lot. No planned planting has been added except to enhance the natural forest.

Quarry tile floors the double-story solarium/gallery, designed for plants and paintings. Georgia artists represented in the Steeds' collection are Ben Smith, Alan Tiegreen, Dorothy Mizell, Anthony Rice, Dan Poole and potter Pat Suttles.

The gallery forms the shape of an "H," crossed by two bridges leading to the bedrooms and Mrs. Steed's painting studio. Moroccan rugs are used extensively throughout, but the one seen hanging over the balcony railing was hand-woven in Mexico.

Soft blue cotton slipcovers and a sandy beige rug soften and lighten the dramatic dark beams and woodwork in the poolside sitting room of Mr. and Mrs. J. Scott Crabtree.

"I love flowers," says Sissie Crabtree, "and this is one room where you can have zinnias."

Furniture from a Manhattan apartment and a summer house in Oyster Bay, Long Island, was combined for casual living in the somewhat formal setting of this West Andrews Drive home.

The picture of the child with the black dog, painted years ago by Ebet Roberts, a native of Scott Crabtree's home town, Memphis, Tennessee, bears a fortuitous likeness to the Crabtrees' daughter, Laura.

In the master bedroom, scalloped linens from France and a quilt from the Memphis Women's Exchange combine ingeniously. An old French découpage chest at the foot of the bed serves an everyday function, holding bulky sweaters and mufflers. The pine Adam-style mantel and walnut pier mirror are English antiques.

A terrace in softly-colored Saint Joe brick echoes the reddish roof tiles of the studio wing in the home of Atlanta artist Comer Jennings.

The studio, designed by Otto Zenke to complement the Tudor style house, has leaded glass windows looking onto the terrace garden and the woods beyond. An old French farm table and a Parsons table hold paints and brushes.

In a contrasting mood, a severe English Windsor chair and a functional architect's table lend great dignity and character to the living room.

From top left across: Dogwoods and azaleas surround the entrance to the Colonial-inspired house of Mrs. Lon W. Grove. A wrought-iron gate was original to her childhood home, the J.J. Haverty residence, formerly on Peachtree Road…"Butterfly Manna," with its colonnaded portico, is home to Mr. and Mrs. Bert Lance…Stately oaks complement the Georgian façade of the Julian Barfield house. A fanlight and a classic arch supported by Doric columns surmount the doorway. The pediment is upheld by simplified Corinthian columns.

Center, left to right: The playhouse in the garden at the home of Mrs. Malcolm Fleming…Whorls of fanciful wrought iron in a garden gate… Mimosa Hall, family home of the Edward C. Hansells, is one of the stately "great halls" of the town of Roswell. Due north of Atlanta, Roswell predates the larger city by several years and includes some homes older than Atlanta itself.

Bottom from left: Fanlights over ground floor windows and entrance to the home of Mrs. William Schroder are echoed in arched detail over an enclosed porch…Greens—lime and apple—keynote a sunny seating area in the home of Dr. and Mrs. David Cohen …Neel Reid, a gifted architect working in Atlanta and Georgia during the first quarter of this century, enhanced his gracious traditional houses with comfortable porches, such as the one at bottom right, an integral part of the Emory Schwall home. The Schwalls have turned the loggia created by the arched colonnade into a glass-enclosed year-round garden room.

Not long after Mr. and Mrs. James L. Bentley, Jr., were married, they drove past a quaint old house, boarded up and neglected. "Wouldn't it be wonderful if it could be restored?", they said.

Ten years later, it was for sale, restored by architect Kennon Perry in 1955. Thrilled, they bought it and furnished it lovingly with antiques.

The house is the oldest building in Atlanta and stands now in a graceful "close-in" neighborhood of wide streets, spacious homes and well-kept lawns. The area was described as a

"trackless wilderness" by Meredith Collier, who built the house in 1822, long before Atlanta was even a gleam in a surveyor's eye. His son, George Washington Collier, planted a walnut tree in the yard when he was thirteen, in 1825. The tree still stands near the old smokehouse.

More than 100 years later, young Samuel Jackson Bentley found a Minié ball lodged in the wall of the smokehouse. It dated from the Battle of Atlanta in 1864.

It has long been said among architects that "There is nothing to astonish about classical architecture, as it is not built to astonish but to please." The geometric balance and foursquare character of the Georgian façade of the home of Mrs. Charles B. Nunnally is lightened by subtle ecru-green on brick and trim. The delicate iron balustrade and brass coach lanterns are relevant details.

The formal shaping of the hedge is balanced by flowering crabapple, pear

and peach trees that add springtime color to the grounds. Built in 1932 by architect Dan Bowdeen, the house was later enlarged to include a garden room.

Classic columns and an arched doorway lead guests into a dramatic reception hall flanked by a gracefully curving staircase. The hall gives access to living and dining areas, as well as the garden room. A bright bouquet and a curtain treatment by interior designer David Byers soften lines of classic simplicity.

Dr. and Mrs. Joseph M. Gibson collected architectural fragments for years before commissioning architect Jerry Garrison to build their home. He used entry doors found in Florence, Italy, as the focal point of a house with a country French flavor.

Mrs. Gibson, a talented designer, and her associate Jerry Underwood have used an antique Heriz rug to underscore the red and blue scheme in the living room. Sophisticated accessories add punch. Brackets supporting the beams are from Governor John Slaton's house, once on Peachtree Road.

Edith Hills has enjoyed a sparkling career as an interior designer in Atlanta for more years than some would wish to count. When asked to describe herself, she laughingly replies, "Octogenarian!"

Her vibrant colors and sure hand with luxurious fabrics defy fadism. Trademarks are whimsical accessories played against a Continental look, plenty of silk, and subtly painted finishes, all a little rococo and very feminine.

In her own "cottage," French casement windows and a glassed roof let morning sun into the "fern room" and brighten the table, draped in a Chinese silk of pale lacquer yellow. A collection of books on decoration and furniture, many out of print, makes a library used by Mrs. Hills' staff, clientele and friends. Chairs are Italian with a painted finish, the seats covered with embroidered linen with celadon green background and blue flowers, echoing the Chinese porcelain temple jars topping the étagère.

An old Chinese robe, stretched on a rod and serving as a wall-hanging, is a great throw-away luxury touch in the Hills' style. Its dainty colors are repeated in a striped paneling alternating dusty blue and an antique rose-red. The room's trill of color is topped by a charming chandelier of Parisian design, an ormolu cage containing a collage songbird.

In the home of Mr. and Mrs. Dudley B. Pope, nautical blue and white make a jaunty combination for a poolside room that can serve as a party suite or—with its pullman kitchen and adjoining bath—as a complete guest apartment. An antique walnut armoire (not shown) serves as a guest closet, fitted with rods for hanging and a small batik chest for folded clothes.

As vice president in charge of display and design ("everything visual") for Rich's, Inc., Dudley Pope was one of the

first Atlanta designers to make extensive use of natural materials and green plants. This room, with its sisal carpet, wicker furniture and towering scheffelera, reflects his style.

A navy blue zippered canvas sofa cushion and batik pillows echo the color of the rear wall. The painting over the mantel, "Low Tide" by Roxanna Sway, "reminds us of every beach we've ever been to." Inside shutters of woven matting fold back or close completely to shut out light.

Large oaks and graceful dogwood trees shade the expansive front lawn of the home of Mr. and Mrs. William T. Healey.

This American Colonial style house was built in 1936 on Vernon Road. It was designed for the Healeys by Atlanta architect Philip Shutze.

The previous decade had been marked by numerous projects of American architectural research and restoration, notably in the historic city of Williamsburg, Virginia, which was begun in 1926. Contemporary with the Williamsburg re-construction came the restorations of Monticello and Stratford Hall, the home of General Robert E. Lee, also in Virginia.

The work sparked a general interest in the early architectural history of this country, and architects and designers largely abandoned the European influences popular in the earlier part of the Twentieth Century in favor of a return to Colonialism.

By 1936, the Egleston Spring Tour of Homes had begun to include interiors in addition to gardens. The Healey home, for which Edith Hills served as interior designer, was among the first to open its doors.

A conically-roofed round tower keep dominates the exterior of the home of Mr. and Mrs. Richard Leigh Kattel. Recalling an English manor house with Norman features, it is built of stucco with stone trim and a grey tile roof. Wide casement windows let in plenty of sunshine, dispelling any traces of "castle gloom."

There is a saying: "If you would be happy for a week, marry. If you would be happy for a month, buy a ham. If you would be happy forever—plant a garden."

The original owner of the Kattel house, Mr. Roger Wilby, was a noted gardener. In the 1920s, he brought in an English gardener, trained at Kew Gardens (the Royal Botanical Gardens) near London. He built a greenhouse and extensive rock gardens and supervised the staff that maintained them. Exceptional and rare plantings he installed included Scottish stock rhododendrons and Japanese iris bulbs.

When the Kattels bought the house some years ago, they were intrigued by evidences of the old gardens and began clearing underbrush from around many of the surviving azaleas and retracing and restoring the old rock garden borders. They have been rewarded by a resurgence of many of the plants, grateful for light and air once again.

The old greenhouses across the road are gone, as the property has been divided and many later houses, some larger than their older neighbors, now line the old drive. Each spring the decades-old camellia bushes blossom afresh.

A family portrait from the turn of the century, hung over the antique pine mantel, was the inspiration for this living room for Mr. and Mrs. Neal Irby. Housed here are three English oak lowboys, a pine corner cupboard filled with Toby jugs, and Windsor chairs made of pine, yew and elm. The walnut Queen Anne bench in front of the fireplace rests atop a Greek needlepoint rug. Chairs are upholstered in a tree of life Liberty print, used in conjunction with a natural linen on the sofa.

Plants abound in the master bedroom that features a quilted throw on the chaise and matching bed quilt made by Mrs. Irby in the "Dresden Plate" pattern. Natural shutters at the windows blend with the stripped and refinished mantel, original to the house, that shows off more of the owner's talent, the handpainted tiles. A portrait from Scotland hangs over the mantel.

Staffordshire pieces are used in the room, along with the English brass seat fender at the fireplace and a Greek needlepoint rug.

In the course of their travels, the Simon Selig family have collected sculptures of Rodin and Maillol, as well as a large number of paintings. Clockwise from top left above the sofa are works by Mondoff, Robert Vickery, Vu Cao Dam, Louis Valtat, Henri Martin and Fernand Léger. A work by Jean Jansem is in the center.

Chinese porcelains, English Regency furniture and handsome egg-and-dart mouldings combine felicitously in the curve of the stairwell. Elsewhere, an elaborate escritoire holds an assortment of small "collectibles."

The townhouse of Mr. and Mrs. John Goodloe offers a handsome example of a new Atlanta residential trend—clustered homes in a secluded setting. It is a part of Townsend Place, a community of townhouses set in rolling woodlands near the Chattahoochee River.

The house is built of old brick and recalls 18th Century architecture with its arched fanlight doorway, and shuttered windows, which have twelve over twelve panes on the ground floor and nine over twelve above.

Although each Townsend Place residence has its own private entrance, Mrs. Goodloe designed her own plantings to further personalize her home and create a welcoming terrace garden.

A jolly Chinese musician welcomes guests from high atop his perch in the garden room. The armoire is painted in Mrs. Goodloe's favorite citrus and sunshine colors to combine with crisp cotton slipcovers in a tangerine and lemon print on the wicker chairs. The treillage pattern of the wallpaper further contributes to the garden atmosphere.

Dark verdigris-green glazed walls and mantelpiece make a rich background for an extensive collection of Southern books and memorabilia in the library of Mr. and Mrs. James Graham Kenan. The red leather chair and Canterbury stand for magazines form a cozy fireside spot for reading.

A cannon model on the desk leads the eye to the portrait of General Robert E. Lee, Commander-in-Chief of the Army of the Confederacy. This tinted lithograph is one of a limited edition sold throughout the South shortly after Lee's death. The proceeds were used to finance the recumbent statue of Lee installed as a memorial in the chapel of Washington and Lee University in Lexington, Va. General Lee is buried, along with other members of his family, in this chapel which he built and in which he worshipped while president of the school, then called Washington College.

In the Kenan library, a pair of porcelain figures of General Lee and his most trusted subordinate, General Thomas Jonathan "Stonewall" Jackson, accompany numerous volumes on the Confederacy's campaigns and history. A well-known English sculptress of equestrian statues, Catherine Wheeler, created the models for the statuettes, and they were sold at the time of the Civil War Centennial. Behind the porcelain generals is a photograph of the President of the Confederacy, Jefferson Davis.

A high-ceilinged space can be expansive and soothing and, at the same time, livable and warm. Proof is here in the elegant, yet relaxed, home of Mr. and Mrs. Rhodes Perdue.

Reflected light from the Chattahoochee River floats into the creamy spaces and punctuates the Coromandel screen that accompanies the collection of porcelains. A pair of ivory tusks, trophies from an African hunt, arch into the painted beams and add their coloring to the monochromatic scheme of beiges, whites and wood tones. A natural flagstone platform provides an interesting change in both texture and elevation and leads the eye to the dining room beyond.

The screen, on its walnut stand, is glimpsed again in the gently columned mirror above the French mantel at the opposite end of the room. Chinese vases flank a bust of son David Perdue, at age five, by Belgian sculptor Jean Gaevert.

The late afternoon sun dapples the Palladian-style residence of Mr. and Mrs. Claude P. Brown. Unique columned porticos flank the main block. The house was designed by Atlanta architect Philip Shutze and built in 1929 by Charles Black, the developer of Tuxedo Park.

For many years it was home to Mr. and Mrs. Robert T. Jones. He was better known as "Bobby"—the most celebrated of golfing greats.

Jones won 13 major golf championships and climaxed his career by winning the Grand Slam of golf: the United States Open, the British Open,

the United States Amateur and the British Amateur Tournaments. The year was 1930. Jones was 28.

On his return to Atlanta, instead of giving Bobby the keys to the city, the town fathers gave the young married man a bungalow. In a few years it became too small for the growing family and this house, "Whitehall" on Tuxedo Road, was purchased.

The Browns generously lent their home in 1978 for the Decorators' Show House, an annual showcase of local designers that benefits the Atlanta Symphony Orchestra.

To look at this dramatic room, one might not believe that it is in a once-neglected and aging Atlanta house.

Atlanta architect Stanley L. Daniels described his decision to remodel a half-century old one-story bungalow rather than to design his own home in an interview in <u>Interior Design Magazine</u> in March, 1972:

"The old house was of considerably less than nondescript design. However, it was located in a section of Atlanta that is extremely convenient both to the business district and to outlying areas—a section my partners and I had been interested in revitalizing."

The living room, pictured here, was dark and cramped. Daniels removed the front porch that kept out the light, substituting a brick-paved glass-walled garden room. In addition, he opened the ceiling into the former attic space, installing more glass to close the gable end. These changes gave both dramatic dimension and light, as well as a relation to the outside trees and new entry courtyard.

Daniels then conceived the bold linear supergraphics to emphasize the new spaciousness, doing the real work himself. With architect John Busby, another partner in the firm of Jova/Daniels/Busby, he designed the tapestry which hangs over the custom-built music cabinet. The raised block coffee table is another Daniels design.

The furnishings are kept simple, giving the stage to the graphics and art which, in turn, form a dramatic foil for people in the room. First built as a bachelor domain, the house now accommodates a young family.

In the south-facing sun room of Mrs. Arthur Lucas, Atlanta designer William Rudolph used white on the woodwork to emphasize a dramatic color scheme of Persian blue-green and the pink-tinged "Dorothy Draper red." Black and white tiled floors and white rattan furniture augment the impression of crispness and light.

The Lucas home is one of the few residences remaining on Peachtree Road that has not undergone some change in form or function. Its Classic Revival design in rosy-pink brick is elegant in its

simplicity. The entry, where groups of Corinthian columns support a porch with handsomely detailed moulding and a delicate iron balustrade, makes an effective center for a balanced façade.

Designed by architect Thornton Marie for Mr. Hollins Randolph in the 1920s, it is copied in part from an early 18th century house in Virginia belonging to the Randolph family. Owned by the Lucases since 1935, it serenely ignores the rush of Peachtree traffic.

A drive of river pebbles provides a rustic approach to the home of Mr. and Mrs. Lloyd T. Whitaker. The siding, which is stained a dark black-brown, and the weathered shingle roof are brightened by crisp white trim. The Cape Cod house was designed by James Means.

The house is on the site of the Civil War Battle of Peachtree Creek, which took place July 20, 1864, and ended in disaster for the South. Historical markers in the area trace the course of events.

As described by John F. Stegeman in the Atlanta Journal's "Battles of Atlanta," October 14, 1978: "A suicidal Confederate charge was ordered by audacious General John B. Hood, who only the day before had replaced General Joseph E. Johnston as commander of the Southern defenders. Hood, ready for a blaze of glory, rashly determined to drive back the Federal command, which had advanced and threatened the railroad center of Atlanta.

"The rebel yells of the attacking Southerners blended with screams of the wounded, as column after column of Confederates were decimated as they came pouring down to the creek. When it was over, five thousand Confederate dead and wounded lay strewn across the battlefield, commingled with two thousand casualties of the entrenched Federal troops. This tragic day of bravado broke the spirit of the South."

To this day, residents of the area still find Minié ball bullets and other relics of the battle when they turn ground for planting.

From top left across: Brilliant pink water lilies float in a reflecting pool at the foot of a classic Doric-columned pavilion in the garden of Mrs. Bolling Jones…Afternoon sun dapples the lawn and white brick façade of Mrs. Fonville McWhorter's house. The Georgian fanlight and pediment over the entrance are enlarged in the roof line.

Center, left to right: Traditional pieces combine felicitously with a koa wood buffet server and storage wall in the balconied dining room of Mr. and Mrs. Don Comstock. Sunlight streams through skylights, while a copper chandelier, a stylized artichoke designed by Paul Henningsen, floats above the table…A profusion of springtime tulips bloom in Atlanta's woodland gardens…Twin Dutch Colonial façades mark the home of civic leader Ivan Allen, Jr., and his wife, the former Louise Richardson. Allen was honored for his courage as mayor in guiding Atlanta through the turbulent Sixties.

From bottom left across: The striking English Tudor residence at bottom left belongs to Mr. and Mrs. Wiley P. Ballard, Jr. The house and grounds, along with numerous other northwest Atlanta homes, were damaged by a tornado which swept through the area in 1975. Painstaking restoration is almost completed…The home of Mr. and Mrs. Frank Carter sits back from the street in a stand of tall pines…A graceful swan in the form of a white porcelain tureen gazes toward the city from the penthouse patio of Mr. and Mrs Frank Ferst in downtown Atlanta. Boxwood plantings are clipped in topiary forms.

A round central skylight and triangular openings formed by the roof's fan-like folds admit light dramatically into the garden room of Mr. and Mrs. Cecil A. Alexander.

Mr. Alexander, a noted architect, has headed numerous prominent projects in the Atlanta area, including the Coca-Cola USA building and the Phipps Plaza retail mall. When he designed his own home, the garden room space was originally conceived as an open inner courtyard. As plans progressed, however, he decided to add an enclosing roof, which functions like an enormous sculpture, letting the outdoor views and lights come in.

Since the flagstone floor is very near ground level, a group of tropical philodendrons could be placed in an indoor tree well. Without restraint for their roots, they have grown sleek and massive, providing another sculptural form.

While most of the furnishings are modern, chosen for this contemporary home, a few cherished family pieces add warmth and provide continuity with the past. The piano and its companion music stand came from Mrs. Alexander's family home in New Orleans. There her family gathered around the piano for impromptu concerts, her father using the stand, which he made himself, as he played the viola. The sense of family tradition is further heightened by a miniature of Mrs. Alexander's mother, placed on one of the candlestands of the piano.

The flagstone floors lead past an indoor garden to the living and dining room, furnished with low modern pieces that do not obstruct the view of the treetops beyond.

The home of Mr. and Mrs. Jack C. Fraser is a favorite of springtime photographers. The garden, with its natural glen planted with native azaleas and dogwood, was designed by William C. Pauley. Huge oak trees frame the house, created by Atlanta architect Neel Reid.

Reid's first concern in the design of any house was its siting. Deep lawns that slope gently toward the street were preferred. The setting of the Fraser house provides a prime example.

Stephen P. Fricano recently purchased this house, which was designed by Atlanta architect James Means. Inspired by a French country house near Vezeley in Burgundy, it features characteristic arched dormer windows set into a mansard roof of weathered wood. Working shutters of solid panels flank the ground floor windows. The vine-covered exterior is of natural stucco.

Wood used in construction, both inside and outside the house, was salvaged from an old warehouse in  downtown Atlanta. Such old buildings, built of nearly indestructible heart pine, are prime sources for the wide board floors and carved woodwork which give the gentle illusion of age to many Means houses. Beams that once bore the weight of mule harnesses or cotton bales now make graceful cornices and window boxes, burnished floors or painted ship-lap paneling.

"It's a shame," said James Means, "to think how we wasted some of that beautiful wood—in attics, for example—and now it's so hard to find."

A deck with flowering plants and an eating area shaded by a sunshine yellow awning almost doubles the space of the family room in the home of Mr. and Mrs. Richard Bell. A large rattan couch in a bright abstract print provides plenty of room for lounging. The scoop-shape chair in the foreground was bought in Taiwan when the Bells lived there some years ago. The dresser, of old pine, is an English antique. The bold wall graphic is by Atlanta artist Barbara Brozik.

An imaginative mix of Oriental and Oriental-inspired objects gives a light touch to the living room, which was decorated by Mrs. Bell. An English Brighton pavilion mirror with curio shelves and the Chippendale open armchair are European styles influenced by the Chinese. Among the true Oriental accessories are the ginger jar, used as a base for the lamp, and the wall scroll, a calligraphic rendering of a graceful bamboo branch. The scroll was given the Bells as a farewell gift by friends in Taiwan.

A pair of majestic stone eagles spread their wings and stand sentinel at the entrance to the home of Mr. and Mrs. Robert F. Bryan on Habersham Road. The wall and façade were copied by architect Neel Reid from Tintinhull House in Somerset County, England.

According to James Grady, author of Architecture of Neel Reid in Georgia, Tintinhull was a small Medieval manor built about 1600 and remodeled about 1720, during the reign of George I. Its classical features—the pedimented center pavilion with pilasters and the entrance doorway with engaged Tuscan columns supporting a curved pediment—are Italian Renaissance, but the mullioned and transomed casement windows from the preceding period were left intact. When Reid designed this Atlanta house in 1918, he incorporated this seeming idiosyncracy from the original.

The windows add an informal charm and country feeling to what might be considered a severe exterior. Large windows and doors were a Reid trademark, a means to gain scale and give an immediate impression of a house of unusual space and size. The walls are of limestone and the entrance court is made of granite setts paved in concentric circles.

Huge oaks surround the house, and the English boxwoods that flank the drive are over fifty years old. The boxwood garden for the house was designed by students at the University of Georgia, working with noted landscape architect Hubert Owens, as a student project in the Department of Landscape Design.

This hilltop home of Mr. and Mrs. Wayne M. Watson, built in 1925, was the final work of noted Georgia architect Neel Reid. It was copied from the Hammond-Harwood house in Annapolis, Maryland, itself the final work of architect William Buckland in 1774.

The entrance door, considered one of the finest of American 18th Century design, has engaged Ionic columns and pediment. Sweeping lawns and azalea plantings surround the house, while stately old trees and a stream frame the view from the front drive.

Yellow glazed walls give a sunny look to the morning room. A many-branched Waterford chandelier and a baroque mirror catch the light from the high arched windows.

A needlepoint rug in a soft Chinese design is framed by black and white marble floors. The couch in a "tobacco leaf" print is foil to mahogany antique furniture. The portrait is of Admiral Vernon, under whose command George Washington served, and for whom Washington's home Mt. Vernon is named.

The bright red door, yellow banister and cheerful geranium pots that accent the traditional façade of the Anthony M. Ames house all hint of surprises inside.

Ames, an Atlanta architect, renovated this 1920's home to let in the light. Skylights, large solid sheetglass windowpanes and lots of white paint conspire to create wide, airy spaces.

Le Corbusier prints and chairs key a dramatic loggia, and the plum Mies van der Rohe chairs in the dining room exemplify the less-is-more esthetic of the Ames house.

Although built in the 1930s, the Robert W. Woodruff house, with its triangular pediment, ornamental pilasters and medallions, harks back to a much earlier era of magisterial classicism. Its owner, for fifty-five years a member of the board of directors of The Coca-Cola Company, and since 1955 chairman of its finance committee, is recognized as one of America's pre-eminent industrialists and one of the country's major philanthropists.

The dining room is furnished with a

collection of formal English antique furniture, and graced by a portrait of Mrs. Nell Hodgson Woodruff.

When the Woodruffs put their home on tour to benefit the Henrietta Egleston Hospital, Mamie Eisenhower, a friend of Mrs. Woodruff's, sent a centerpiece decoration for the table, described in an account by The Atlanta Journal as an arrangement of "lace coral, sea fans, and six exquisite wax hibiscus."

Cooper and Cooper were the architects for this English manor house of stone with its traditional slate roof. Various features were borrowed from "Hever," the home of Anne Boleyn. Shown here is a portion of the boxwood courtyard with additional azalea plantings.

Purchasing the house after it had been damaged by fire, Mr. and Mrs. Edward E. Elson set themselves a dual challenge in restoration—to retain the character of the Tudor architecture and at the same time open the rooms to accommodate modern furnishings and art.

The essential interior character of the house remains in the heavily beamed ceilings and stone fireplace. Large stone-framed arches expand the living room into two adjacent sitting rooms. The flowing pattern of the rug is in marked contrast to the sleek geometry of the stainless steel cocktail table, both designed by Irv Weiner. Plum velvet is used on the sofas and ottoman. The painting above the mantel—Spanish realist Claudio Bravo's "Supermarket"—provides a contemporary focal point.

The Edward Hagen Mattingly home on Argonne Drive nestles deeply into its wooded vale. The design is adapted from 18th Century New England houses and the doorway is an exact copy of the one on the "Parson" Jonathan Ashley house in Old Deerfield, Massachusetts. It was handmade by master-carver William Gass to duplicate the original, dated circa 1730. The simple façade is accented only by the beaded edges of the white clapboards, giving full emphasis to the door. Such doors are one of the most significant architectural features of early Connecticut River houses and appear nowhere else in Colonial architecture.

The exuberant colors in the cheerful back living room also come from Colonial New England. The blue trim is a copy of a color found in the Dwight Barnard house, also in Old Deerfield. A serpentine-back sofa in rich red cotton brocade has cushions of crewel and bargello-stitch woolen handwork. Crewel curtains pick up the blue in beams and mouldings.

Dramatic spring-blooming Kwansan cherry trees front the home of Mr. and Mrs. Julian S. Carr on Northside Drive. Arches of open wooden lattice work line the porch, adding a delicate grace to this 18th century Connecticut farmhouse adaptation, designed by Atlanta architect Philip Shutze in 1939. White dogwood flowers near the house and English boxwood hedges etch the entry courtyard.

A comfortable library with wide "ship-lap" panelled walls, ceiling beams and functional window shutters, all

painted in a soft, creamy gold, forms a pleasant retreat. A long sofa is upholstered in a gold and cream cotton print. A Louis XVI bergére, to the right of the sofa, and a small Louis XV fauteuil by the chest are united by Pompeian red upholstery in complementary fabrics. Two lightly scaled pull-up chairs are placed invitingly near the card table in the bay window, a grouping that works equally well for bridge or conversation. The flower painting is by Atlanta artist Jarvin Parks.